Fly, Butterfly

Brenda Parkes

Some eggs on a leaf
warm in the sun.

They hatch into caterpillars one by one.

The caterpillar eats
and eats and eats.

It turns into a pupa
hanging from a leaf.

Then a butterfly hatches,
and when its wings are dry,

the beautiful butterfly
can fly, fly, fly.

Life Cycle

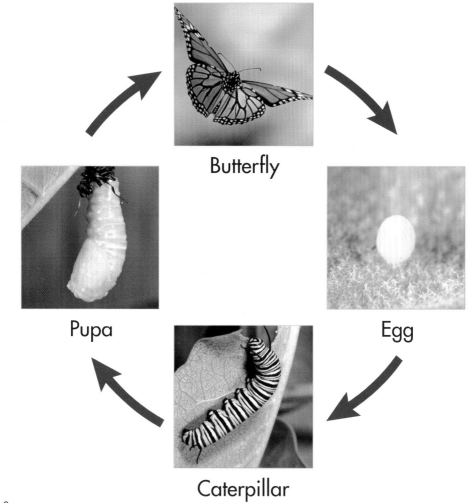

Butterfly

Egg

Caterpillar

Pupa